Banjo's Tall Tales

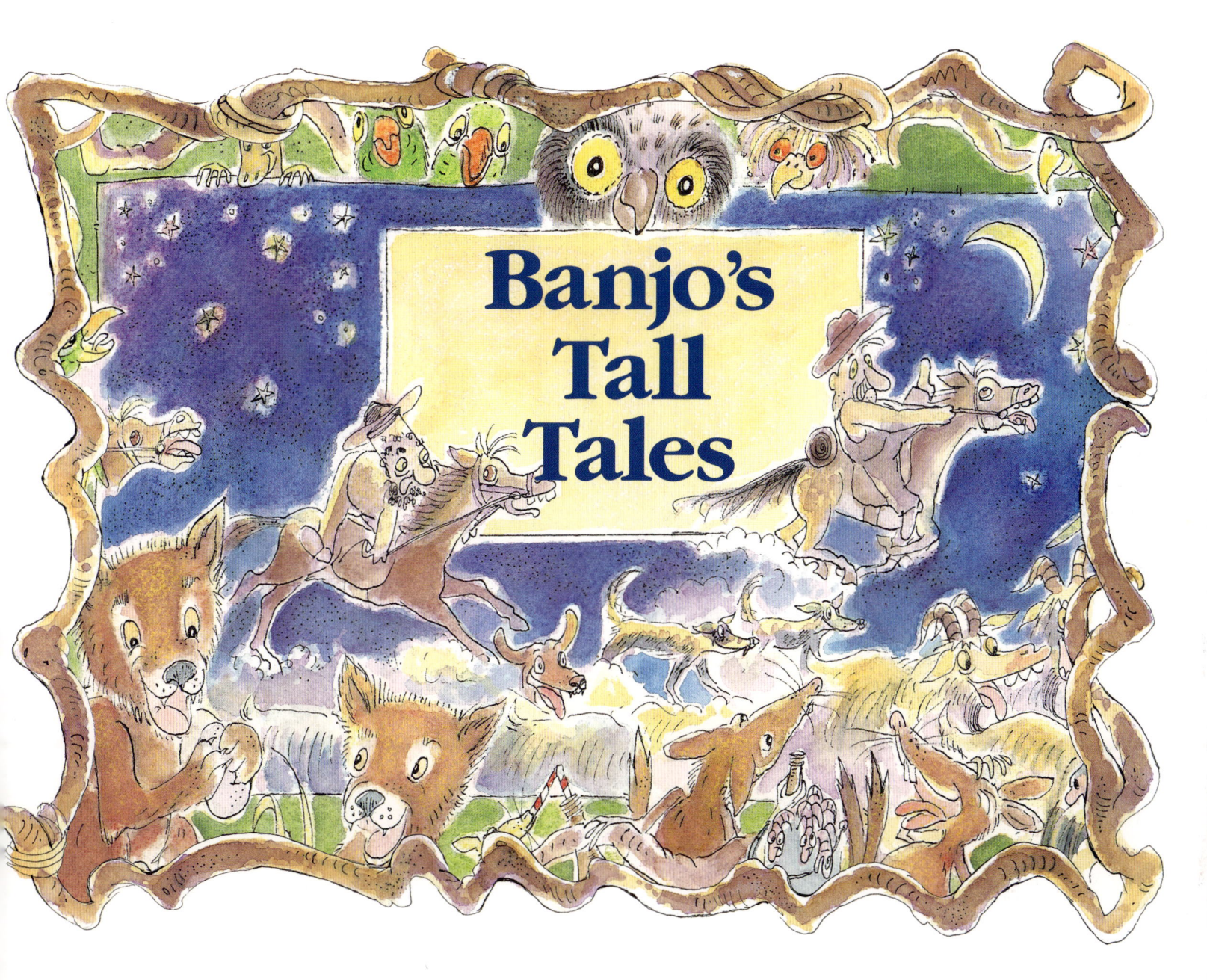

Illustrated by Cheryl Westenberg

Murray Child & Company
an imprint of
MURRAY DAVID PUBLISHING PTY LTD

This book belongs to

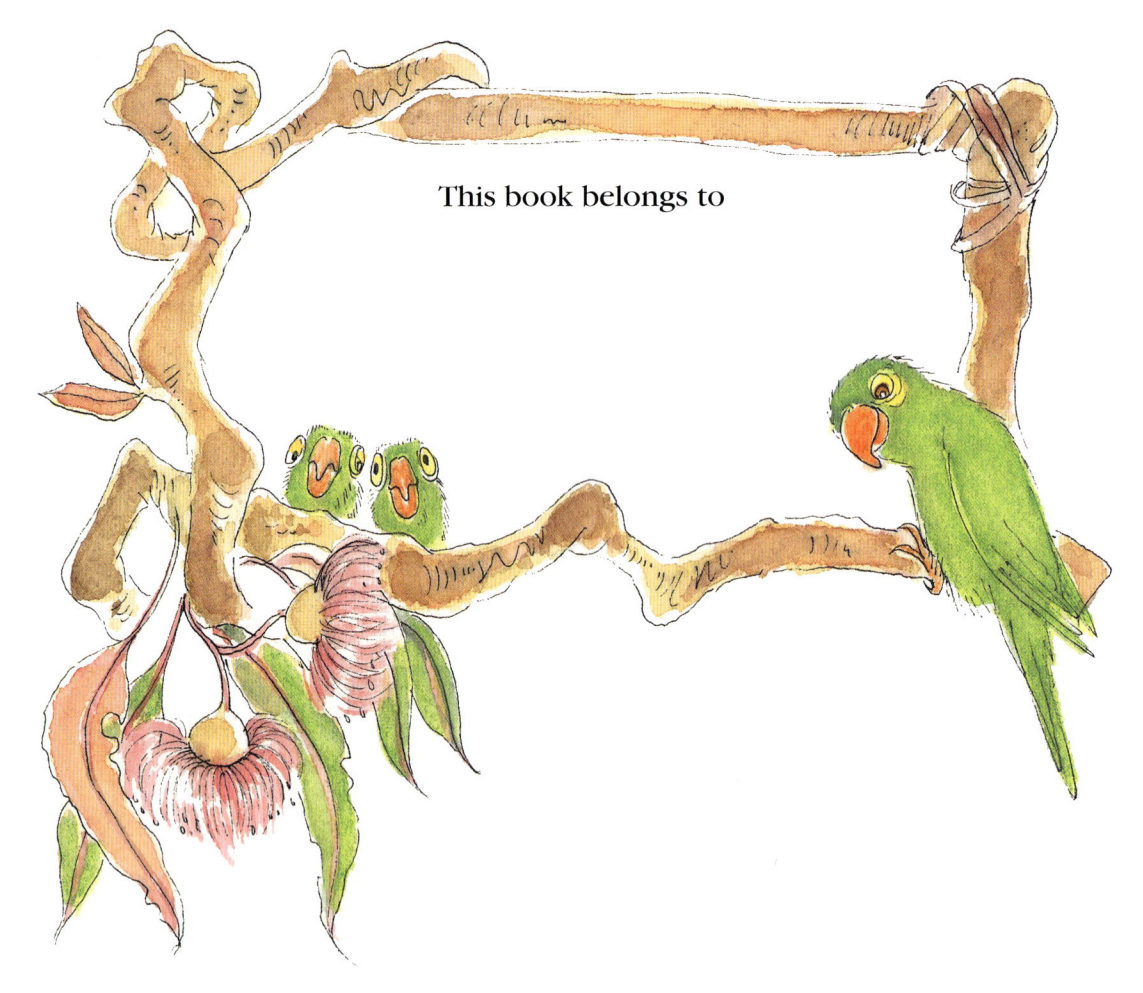

Published by
Murray Child & Company an imprint of
Murray David Publishing Pty Ltd
Publishing: 23 O'Connors Road, Beacon Hill, NSW 2100
Sales and Marketing: 33a Carnarvon Drive, Frenchs Forest NSW, 2086
First published 1998
Typographic design by Emma Seymour
Film by Leo Reprographic
Printed by South China Printing Company

A selection of original poems by A. B Paterson from the Collection
The Animals Noah Forgot first published by The Endeavour Press 1933
© Copyright Murray David Publishing Pty Ltd, 1998

ISBN Hardbpound: 0 908048 37 8
ISBN Paperback: 0 908048 44 0

All rights reserved. No part of this publication may be reproduced,
stored in a retrieval system, or transmitted in any form, or by
any means, electronic, mechanical, photocopying, recording,
or otherwise, without the prior written
permission of the publisher.

Camouflage

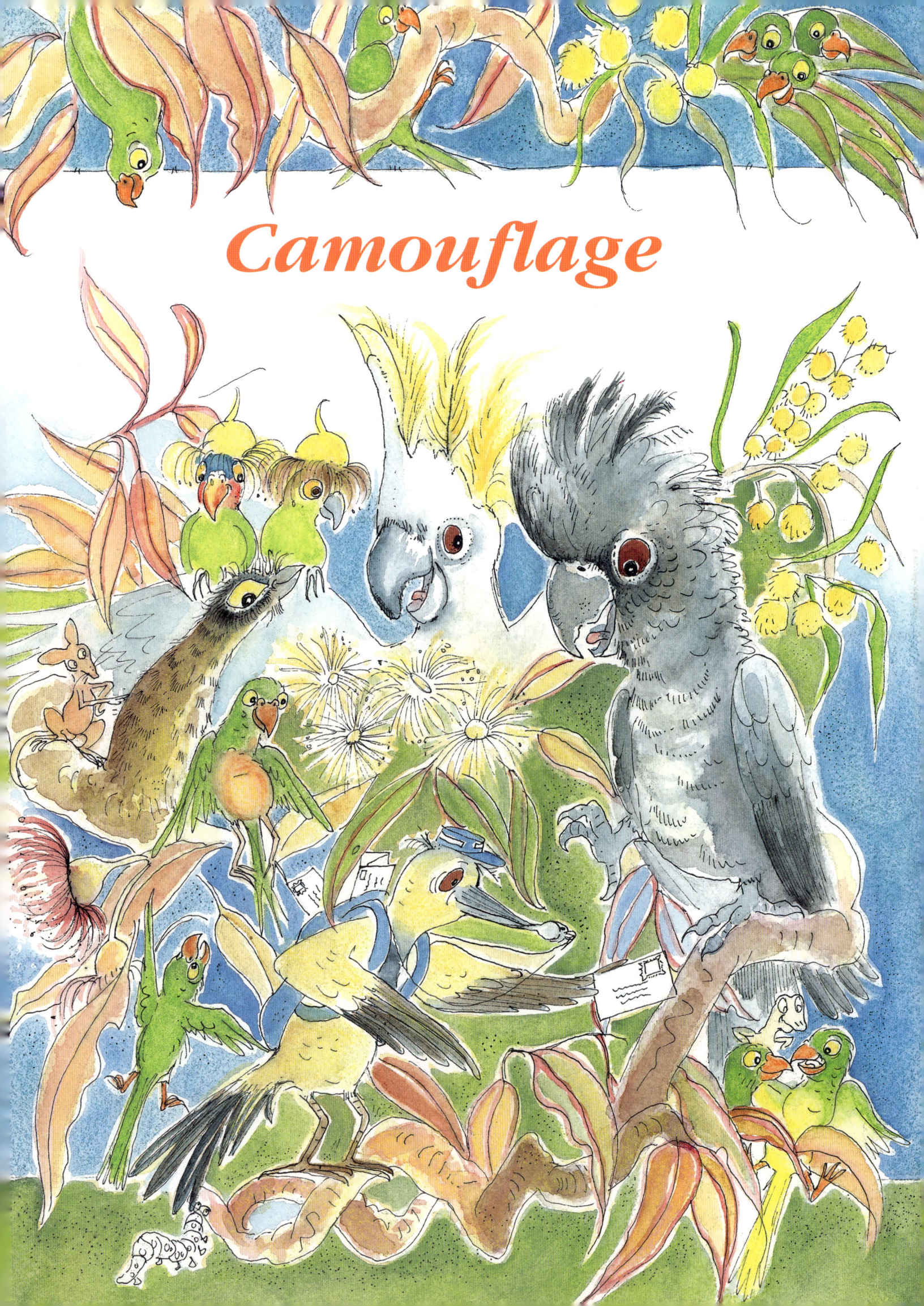

Beside the bare and beaten track of travelling flocks and herds,
The woodpecker went tapping on, the postman of the birds,
"I've got a letter here," he said, "that no one's understood,
Addressed as follows: 'To the bird that's like a piece of wood.'"

"The soldier-bird got very cross
— it wasn't meant for her;

To the Bird
thats like a
piece of wood

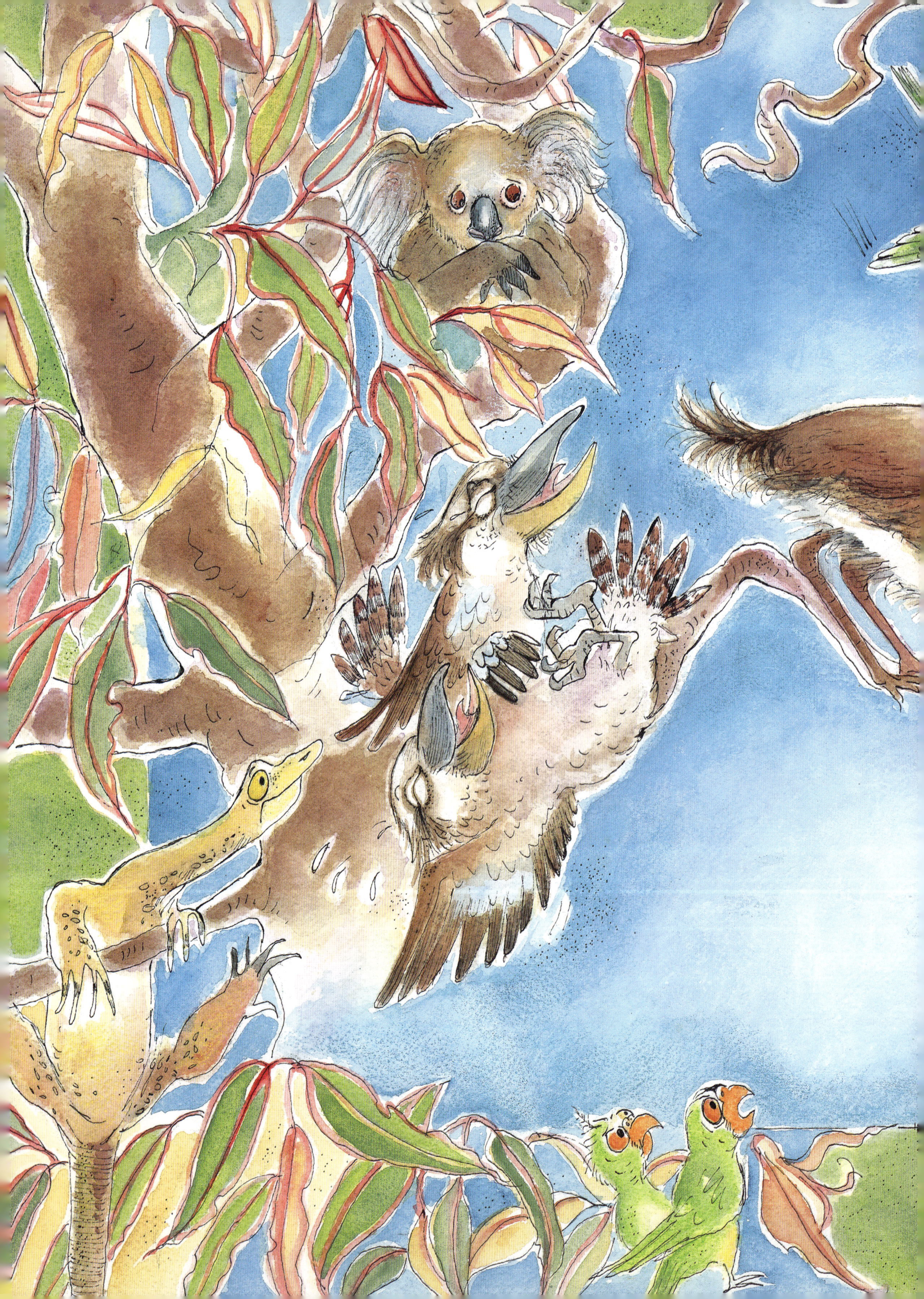

The spurwing plover had a try to
   stab me with a spur;
The jackass laughed, and said the thing
   was written for a lark.
I think I'll chuck this postman job
   and take to stripping bark."

Then all the birds from miles around
came in to lend a hand;
They perched upon a broken
limb as thick as they could stand.

And just as old man eaglehawk prepared to have his say
A portion of the broken limb got up and flew away.

Then, casting grammar to the winds,
  the postman said: "That's him!
The boo-book owl — he squats himself
  along a broken limb,
And pokes his beak up like a stick;
  there's not a bird, I vow,
Can tell you which is boo-book owl
  and which is broken bough.

"And that's the thing he calls his nest — that jerry-built affair —
A bunch of sticks across a fork; I'll leave his letter there.

A cuckoo wouldn't use his nest,
but what's the odds to him —
A bird that tries to imitate a piece
of leaning limb!"

High Explosive

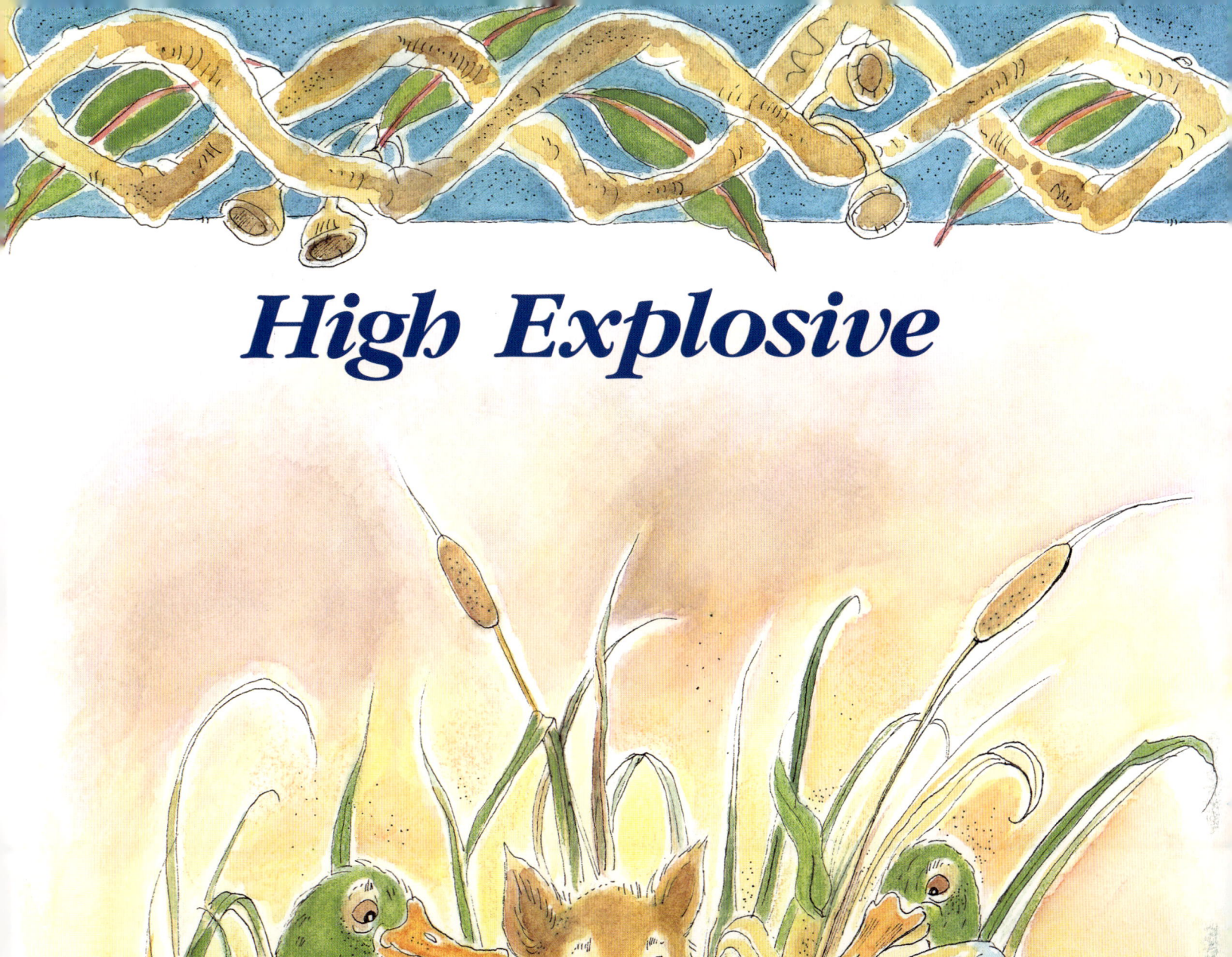

'Twas the dingo pup to his dam that said,
"It's time I worked for my daily bread.
Out in the world I intend to go,
And you'd be surprised at the things I know.

"There's a wild duck's nest in a sheltered spot,
And I'll go right down and I'll eat the lot."
But when he got to his destined prey
He found that the ducks had flown away.

But an egg was left that would quench his thirst,
So he bit the egg and it straightway burst.
It burst with a bang, and he turned and fled,
For he thought that the egg had shot him dead.

"Oh, mother," he said, "let us clear right out
Or we'll lose our lives with the bombs about;

And it's lucky I am that I'm not blown up —
It's a very hard life," said the dingo pup.

Benjamin Bandicoot

If you walk in the bush at night,
In the wonderful silence deep,
By the flickering lantern light
When the birds are all asleep
You may catch a sight of old Skinny-go-root,
Otherwise Benjamin Bandicoot.

With a snout that can delve and dig,
With claws that are strong as steel,
He roots like a pigmy pig,
To get his evening meal,

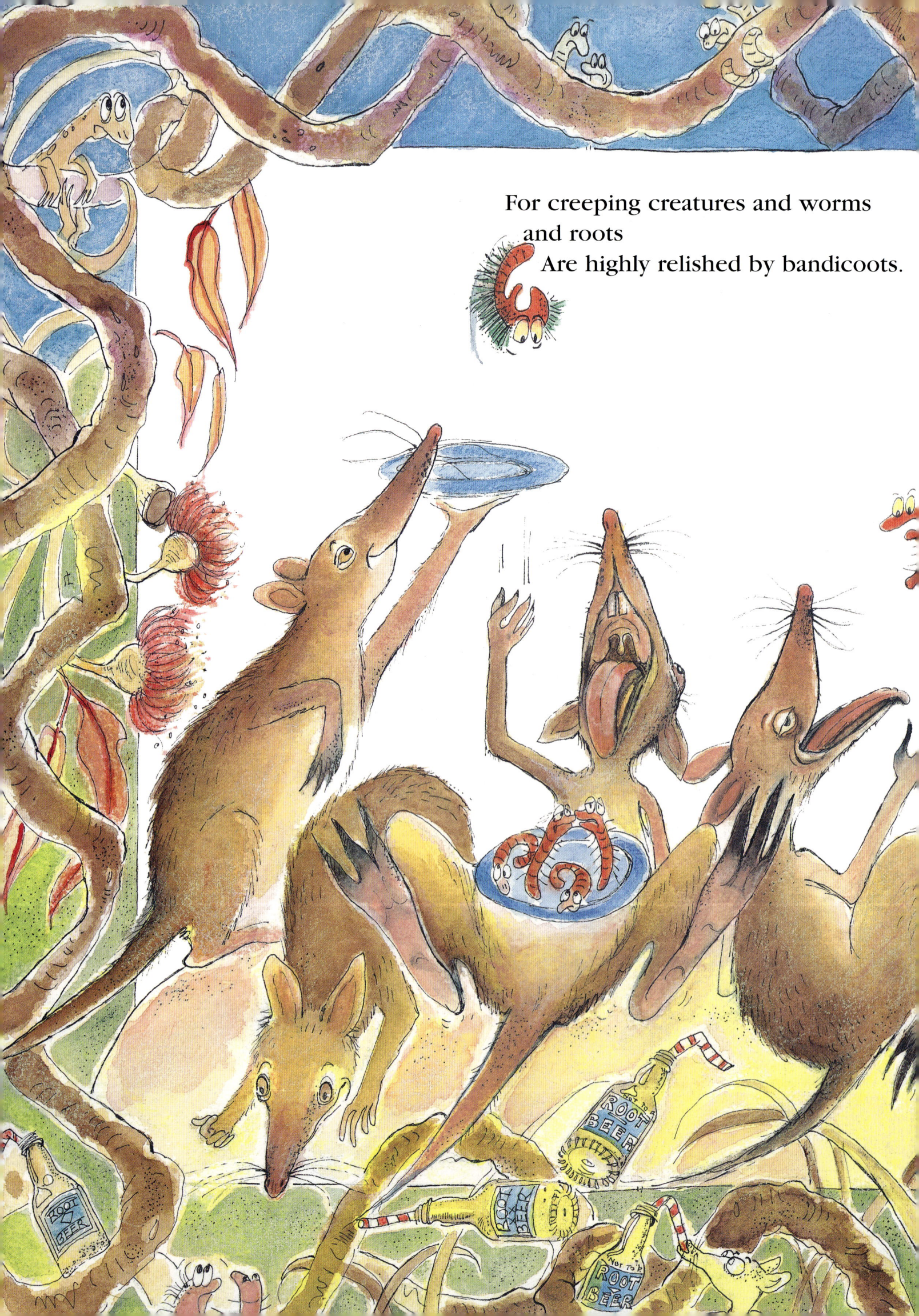

For creeping creatures and worms and roots
  Are highly relished by bandicoots.

Under the grass and the fern
 He fashions his beaten track
With many a twist and turn
 That wanders and doubles back,
And dogs that think they are most astute
 Are baffled by Benjamin Bandicoot.

In the depth of the darkest night,
　Without a star in the sky,
He'll come to look at a light,
　And scientists wonder why:

If the bush is burning it's time to scoot
Is the notion of Benjamin Bandicoot.

The Billy-Goat Overland

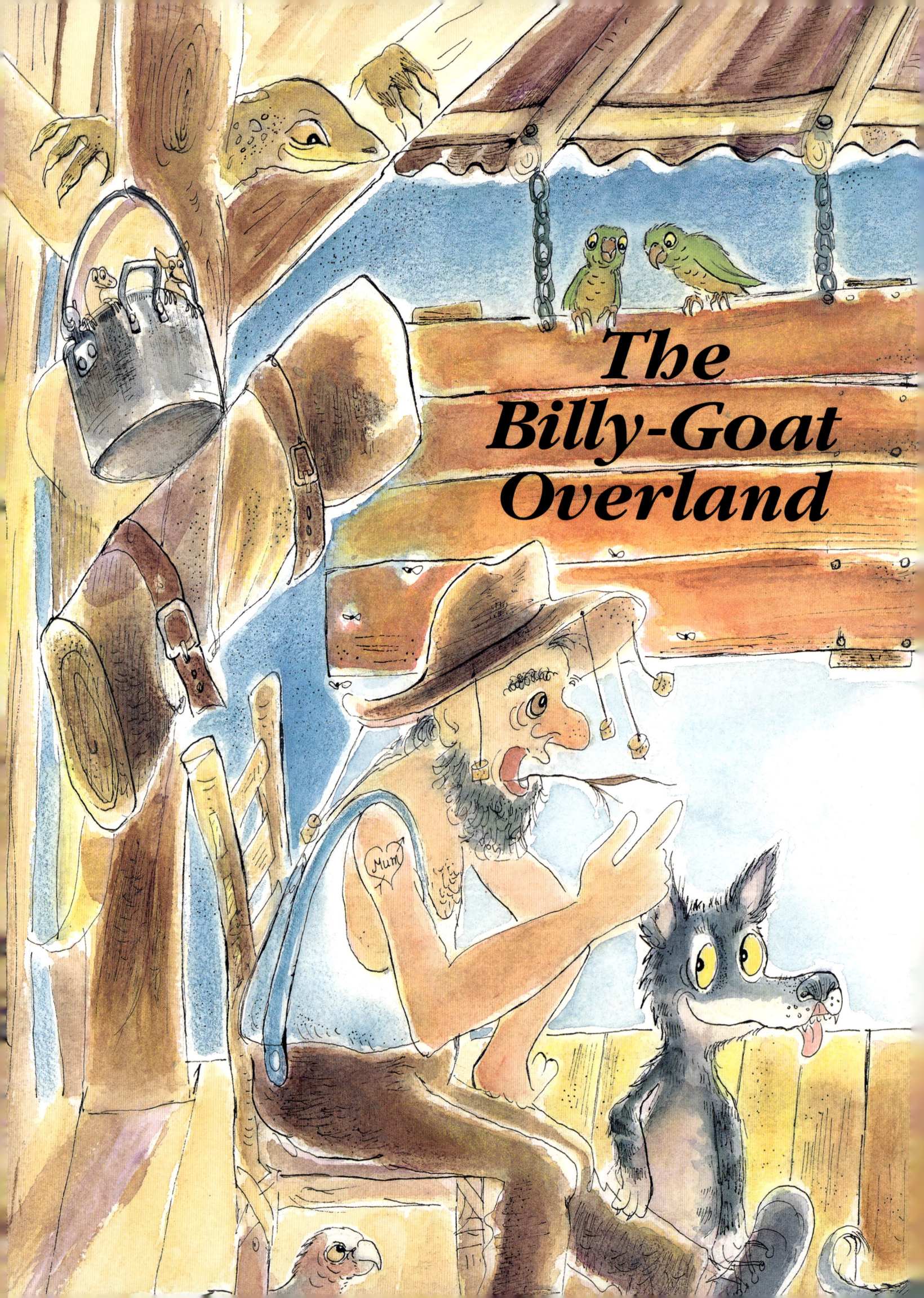

Come all ye lads of the droving days, ye gentlemen unafraid,
I'll tell you all of the greatest trip that ever a drover made,
For we rolled our swags, and we packed our bags,
  and taking our lives in hand,
We started away with a thousand goats,
  on the billy-goat overland.

There wasn't a fence that'd hold the mob, or
  keep 'em from their desires;
They skipped along the top of the posts and
  cake-walked on the wires.

And where the lanes had been stripped of grass and the paddocks were nice and green,
The goats they travelled outside the lanes and we rode in between.

The squatters started to drive them back,
but that was no good at all,
Their horses ran for the lick of their lives
from the scent that was like a wall:

And never a dog had pluck or gall
in front of the mob to stand
And face the charge of a thousand
goats on the billy-goat overland.

We found we were hundreds over strength when we counted out the mob;
And they put us in jail for a crowd of thieves that travelled to steal and rob;
For every goat between here and Bourke, when he scented our spicy band,
Had left his home and his work to join the billy-goat overland.